Karin Lessing

Also by Karin Lessing:

The Fountain
The Spaces of Sleep in Midsummer
The Winter Dream Journals
In the Aviary of Voices

KARIN LESSING

Collected Poems

Shearsman Books
Exeter

Published in the United Kingdom in 2010 by
Shearsman Books Ltd
58 Velwell Road
Exeter
EX4 4LD

ISBN 978-1-84861-131-3
First Edition

Acknowledgements

The work collected in this volume originally appeared in the following books:
The Fountain (New York: Montemora Foundation, 1982),
The Spaces of Sleep in Midsummer (Markesan, WI: Pentagram Press, 1982),
The Winter Dream Journals (Plymouth, Shearsman Books, 1991) and
In the Aviary of Voices (Kentisbeare: Shearsman Books, 2001).

Previously uncollected work in this volume first appeared, or will appear,
in *Shearsman* and *Volt*.

Cover: details from an untitled drawing (pen and ink on paper) by Louis Merveil.
Copyright © The Estate of Louis Merveil, 2010.
The complete drawing appears on page 188.

Cover design: Gilles Fage.
Author photograph by Nathalie Waag.

Contents

The Fountain

III

The Winter Dream Journals

A Winter's Dream Journal

A Winter's Dream Journal II

The Lifelong Range

In the Aviary of Voices

THE FOUNTAIN

Aquesta biua fuente que desseo
en este pan de vida yo la ueo
aunque de noche.
— *St. John of the Cross*

Se faire tout entier signe, c'est
peut-être cela.
—*E. Levinas*

I

Talisman

At the back of the head
a giant
anchors the eyelet sea:

in its jaw, a
bone
is singing: good fortune.

Shadows, firstcomers . . .

Shadows, firstcomers,
sparked and feathered,
you fall, you
dive, driving the spar
into the lung's nest.

No angel, but a maypole,
from crown to
tip toe, swirling
ablaze. How
can the rootless ones
unlock this glow?

Breath, as it winds. I hear
the coronated
heart pod snap,
black, coruscant,
near.

Les Saintes

Braced
the sea wall
and came, outcasts,

to the nacreous edge.

(How
each time we repeat

leaving our imprints,
our

cries: tellina,   tellina).

•

Their salt robes
folded,

votive, on the
burning sand, even
the bottle caps.

The cave, too, burning.

To worship
upon the shore

Sara's
heart,

their shadowy pearl.

Moraine

Through
thyme

braided
to thyme

followed
the scent that

tumbles,
breast-

high, dream-
thin.

Un-
thinking,

saw;
blinded,

heard
how they lie

cluster and
stray,

sometimes
seem to float.

Night Song

Cypress,

night's
needle, my

life's
slow gyre,

long night, long

dawn, the
star-
bristled day.

Hollow Wood

. . .
where
are your rings on
rings: *white*

ripples *white.*
Years,

the bedded stream,
powers

as well as love,
spread

and almost touch.

•

Mountain,
veins
of beating

trace
apart, a-

part the

wind's sleeve

making
music to
a-
bide in.

The Sculptor's Garden

"it is as if they had destroyed beforehand
the words with which one might grasp them"
R.M. Rilke

Frost flowers
in the blaze.

The shattered, the a-
bandoned

grief looks out
sees

I remember, she says

river boats
playfully, the red
and gold drift

exposed,
love's children

(grass
devours wind, rain, time,
all
devouring),

wandering
the stones return

•

As if moss and lichen
were arms

retracting distances.

You,
among the innumerable,
shape loss

•

The work-bridge spins
itself in rust

at the garden's far edge: a
stone resembling sleep,

its
unfinished wing

•

Petrous

How you skim and soar
over
the rainbow you
pull
feather by feather
out of the swollen air.

Quill-gifted,
ramified, the

flight's
structure.

The loss, the
gain: no wick to drain
your stone-
skinned sea.

Luberon

In
your smouldering hip,
mountain,
searching your word:

again.

Miniature

Immensely,
your wrist
    falconer

simple
as winds

flicks,
vaned,
toward prey.

Presage

Drained, the
deep blood cups
a thousand bees.

Damask. Your curtain, eye,
veils, reveals
the dreadful pattern.

Drink. The
indelible, once,
was your first rose.

Le Beaucet: Shadows

Palaces, we
stray, through

one another
move.

Entrances, the
desolate stars,

o ridges
of Montmirail,
your jagged smile.

Follow her
wherever she walks, the

poem.

Like Gliders

in the wind
corridors

words
turn, re-

turn: listen,
watch them

and listen,
wave, their

wings
opening

toward sound,
out

over the pale
wreckage.

Vigil

After the marriage
ceremony's
ingoing, outgoing,
rowing
of voices, vows—

the village *mairie*
like
some cinereous mushroom
of the heart's
intent,
casts off the lamps'
soft shadows.

Numb,
the dial,
the grooved fingers.

Night,
what drives
the brooding,
incessant voices
of love's passage:

night-rovers
circling, black-
ringed.

Il Sogno di Constantino

Dreamer,

your tent
dyed
amaranthine,

is rooted
brightness, the
small flower

each holds,
hand

touching
forehead,

as if
in that space
reflected,

endlessly
opening, all
echoes.

Anabatic

Rock-
drift

high;
higher than

timber; the
heart-
line

stepped,
steps
beyond

towards
what
stone

wizened,
towards
whose

inaccessible
whirr.

Wind-Gathered

Wind-gathered
  the tidal
air
—gathering
crests.

Nightbells'
alarm:

as many rooms as
tongues.

But from the
prairies' glitter
to the estuary:

the grain.

The Barrier

real, un-
real, a colored
flow,

that
explained the color,

but the rocks'
resonance—I still
hear it—

was more than
real.

tossing
the flowering
branch

"without aim or profit"

to see
its lightness, the

amazing
lightness,

grace
in being here

this side
of the oozing
rocks' resonance.

II

Cézanne

White-
washed the new

world of
cars willows

the moving things
we make move

through a savage
stillness—to

urge clay, the
beautiful

branched greens . . .
Watch,

where light
breaks, light's

arrow.

These

reeds: moon-
baskets, your

breath braided them,
cribbed a

dream,   Miriam

Her World
for E. W.

Loosely, the
leaves 'my life

by water' by
air breath-fire and

earth the elemental
upturned boat-

room the simple
wildflowers'

perfect sounds.

From Pliny's Natural History

drop
by drop

the favorite
wild, and

summer
myrrh

•

a handful, 'white
is purest'

says Pliny
cut

from root
to the strongest branches

twice
a year

•

tripartite, one
for the Sun

they drew lots
and the god's due

offered up,
lost;

sometimes
forests of cinnamon

ignite

•

June Poppies

June
poppies

flush
with the road

opening,
shutting,

the pine
mirrors

out
over the fields

the star-
braced shadows:

all
things

under a name.

Through Glass

O, a baby's foot
hop-scotched
on flat tile
these flowerboxes
are tombs

•

Not clay,
desiccated
seed-cakes
currants delectable to Gauls—
that, now, from under
leaves   red
pearling through rock-cleft

•

Earth holds such secrets
that it would keep:
delicate bones
of an adolescent
girl in the womb's
clutches

•

Forget-me-not
that flowers
to think, to
touch . . .
but colorless, to be racked
on that bed

outlasting
like clouds
or dreams   through glass

•

New Oak

for Nina

Eye-
vowel,
sheathed 'o'
of gold

golden lashes
under new
oak
leaf

the eye's
a pianino
light
plays on

moving
softly side-
ways

con-
sonant, as of color
itself.

On the Way

Light then,
only the light   the summer's
last, cling to it.

See,
I'm radiant   and you,
holding it in, are

radiant . . .

Seeds
hum

Arcturus rises,   o you fire-
bearers, you

on the way to ice.

Immortelles

sand
talking to sand

the unfrequent
words'

dunes

•

of this:
sight's fire
furled; a

sea
channelling
inwards

•

dreams'
secret

sun-
lit, lidded

tomb

•

. . . by shadow
to find

the twinned grain
paths

dwindling, a
whisper's

•

Orion's
moved, the

red-
shouldered hill

all wind-
keys

turning
in air

•

Ancestral

rode.
rode you

black sails
from Odessa—

wind, a
toothful
of words

blown
inland,

o ashes: a

place, rock-
rooted,

hooves
to the sea, out

there, in no-
where's

white
white lashing.

Dolls' Houses

I saw
through death's
little door

at Cartier's

the wizened tables,
and chairs.

Nazca

The smallest,
slightest, iridescent
bird, its wing, bill, claw

claws
at the petals'
overhang

these petals
are the gods'

they are
invisible to
men

•

Stones,
stones raked to
reveal lighter ground

making the
naked earth
visible
to the naked eye, saying

step in, step
in is to step out
of the world

•

absorbed
the essence

of claw, of
bill, wing, bird

I choose the
bird for it seems
most
perfect
among the patterns

the way
it imprints shape and
sound,

signalling, signalling the
gap,
flowery

food, drink, dance

•

The plane
glints
in the sun, spins out

in smoke-
tufted straights,
loops

'eternal
love, peace, days'

nor had earth
appeared
more beautiful in its ruins'

luminous web

      of sand, of
      stone, grass, wind.

III

The Image

Archer,
       hubbed

in the cloven
cove

to Samarkand:
your riches,

on trellises
of light:

the pomegranate
—my eye's—

suspended.

Mirror
for Alexandra

You, Lady
with a
pearl, and

you, who
love such things:
ribbons

that curl, the
trickle

of white
acacia—you'd
root

breath's
blossom, thumb

and forefinger
gathering it, to

open, mirror,
your ermine-
edged,

breath-
less

gaze.

Sea-Foam

to hear
again

the bird's
cry

pierce

pierce
and mend

•

leaf, a
knife,

a shadowy reef

blossom,

Mer
de Chine

•

where

sharp
and light

sails
of lobed breath

glide

•

your ridges'
blue, my

barest

news

•

even
the sun-
flower's

black
heart

reminds
me

love moves
also

hate

•

that
from your lips

      it
never
   vanishes

grapes'
purple, sea's
dazzling

foam

•

What It Wants

endless, the
summer sky

darkening
at the edge, the hills

ride
on long shadows

cicada's
in the oak

something, what
is it it wants

wanting
it, grows

like stone
piled onto stone,

stylite,

through
the day

that, still
glittering,

grows

•

Aigues Mortes

Half-blind, half-
seeing
look, there's
nowhere, its

gulls'
litter

where waves, once,
hugged
the puzzled
houses of dream

now walls, now
hushed, lid
upon lid
captive, the

little waters
move—

ripening
in
its blindness, the
shelved salt

towers

•

The Bridge

We entered
wrote ourselves

the runnels. the
white-wristed

bed
flowing under us

caught this, its
resonance

the wild, un-
spoken words'

troughs

•

as if lions
would keep, who,

whose
is there to

keep,
keep us from

grief, a
white

citadel
vanishes

•

though broken forth

I have no voice
to cry the season

the raging marble

the sun

stained   hyacinth.

Pont Flavien, 2 March 1980

September-Wings

A huge, soft
fire
comes

in pyramids
of leaves

days
flaked
with swallows

that austral
tug, all

under
Cassiopea's

steep
crown

•

skies'

scallop, black
lamp

of whistling
leaves

....

not snow
       but swallows

the sudden
shining out of

things that
flock

dip to de-
ploy

taking us
somewhere

like a chime
rings on, then

quiets, the
un-

jewelled
void

•

Nikaia

White bays
innumerable—

the creased
mirrors converge

to fold, hold
you,

caught
in their echoes,

Nike . . . fired

among lilies.

Fontaine

I.

Eye to see sound, sound's
ear of

piled rocks   moss-headed

      these silences

to this, to
that

rock tree
tree rock

      to
covet   your white

voices

II.

black-
blown, springing

from bulb

big as a nail
big as skin
big as sky

hurled,
walking the
sky's

surge

•

into the echo-
web, lush

nest of
same   drawn

sisterly,

drone; the
wave

breaks, a
flutter

of seams
keeps

answering

•

al-
ways,

your voice, your in-
accessible
heart
in the crevasses.

Is it
breath
you want? Tongue,

its reeds,
pellets? Rain
fails.

Drink.
Drink from my snow-

fields.

•

III.

stood here
your hair
in leaves. as if

all
you'll never
know rose
to the edge. bleached,

ate
its way higher, each time,
then

dropped,
leaving its markings

only.
huge mouth, mouth
of the cave,
chasm, rock-

petalled
eye . . . would
purl, lash

the ruin-
risen

world   towards you.

Circle

She-
falcon's cry
circled: to

name   volcanoes
        name   seas

name islands   you'd
be that
rock
raging
alone.

  but the reeds'
lisp   the voices

of children
listing the road . . .

•

byzantine, the
head tucked under
gold

tessarae   of place,
                speech,

unknown song   it changes
you could
not
grasp
it.

. . . whispered
among the reeds, reed-

comb fixed to the lay, eyes
all leaves

underfoot, the
stars, the subtle,
clandestine

here.

Terra Cotta Figures, Villa Giulia

in memoriam D.H. Lawrence

from dark
chambered rock, wide-
eyed, bulb

through the bulbs'
painted door

what spring
steeved you to light, laid

its brightness
about you

•

anche il vento   even as wind

presses the leaf . . .

sunk, half
raised from clay, double-

fluted,
paired. as if they breathed
one another.

. . . on flowered stalks

•

was

what leapt through
your hands, un-

still, plunging ever, wave-
                          seeded

bronze,
in your mirrors,

            the hills',

        wheat

curved
under.

Primavera

papyrus   petals   dust
shredded, their bright clothes
shrouds:

there—nowhere else!—
white ruins   the brown fringed garland
flung, un-

written, *that* flash! and perilous
our own dying, much
being born. Therefore

she rises, green
foam   in which the hills are steeped
and dawn

feathery, your face
as I touched it   flown,
nacreous, the doves'

scooped
waves   I remember the
first step taken, the dark glow—

daughter
of,
wind's pearl, *Primavera,*

then,
stepped on.

The Spaces of Sleep in Midsummer

1.

floss, hirsute
angel   room

wide

to thread
through dormancy

dormancy and light

2.

a bowl, a mat of rushes   wind

                    that rock-
scooper, extravagant

rose

3.

of dawn's
blank sweepings

I speak

    the feral plain

4.

no matter which way you
turn, out-
ward,

into the sea of darkness

                    words,

these scantlings

5.

conch-
shell, a candle

for furnishings

bread,
        that the tree would last

a mouth-
ful
crumbles, o earth

6.

carry me, I'd go
to the edge   of chagrin

leaf-tip   horizon

sea-
green, where it blows

mirror eddying out. tethered

mirage

7.

that it drives, that it
unclenches

snake, I
fable myself

from lavender
to lavender

clasped, the crescent   oils

8.

crow-
shadow,
chandelier

the spaces
of sleep

the spaces of
sleep in midsummer

grow
through my hands

vines,
vines branched

towards thunder

•

THE WINTER DREAM JOURNALS

A Winter's Dream Journal

January 1984

Twilight World Visions

Reading the twilight world visions.
The rock as a gentle shoulder. They were all saying the same thing while clouds gathered to cirrus. This was older than stone, lighter than grass and yet like grass. I cried out in my sleep.

Raspberries, mirabelles . . . ! Raise water, raise it from the well, Mary of Vladimir, star-coiffed one, with your close-fitting hood of antlers! Sprouting from your cheek, the child of Vladimir, redder and paler than magenta rose . . . When I looked up again, the trestled tables were moving away at full speed. An index pointed to where I could not see.

Then it ceased and I whiled away the long day. Angels can still be seen in the refracted colors of the sun's ray.

Naming It

For the coming year, they said, but their voices had already been swept away.

Nearly dry, the Dôa still carries on as if it were a river of some consequence. Its former strength can be guessed at. The wide stretch of cerulean sky between the cliffs on either side is that measure. Only the general staff map and the regional map indicate it running west for about three quarters of its course, taking a sharp turn where it encounters a road and then continuing south-west for a remaining six miles.

D is for daring, *ô* for delight and *a* cascades as *daktylos,* the little finger of surprise, birth, pursuit.

The Chinese Wall

I

The visitors came and stayed on.
I do everything in my power.
The laws of hospitality go back to Abraham's time.

II

A bird's eye view. Kepler was the first to apply the word 'picture' to the reversed image on the retina. With my granulous wings I can reach the city of Shanhaikwan in no time.

III

Say, I want to thread my way across the mountains;
say, I want you to thread your way across the mountains
but: I want me to thread my way across the mountains
you cannot say.

IV

The landscape is not familiar. It is not. Beyond the green fields and buff filament roads leading to impregnable gates, the bustle of streets, a low house facing a courtyard. Orderly, disorderly. A dog tries to drink from the fountain; beyond the gates, the sea with its fictitious horizon.

Good Morning!

Why mornings are dreadful. Why you dread all mornings. Like beginnings. Their multiplicity. Their maze of possibilities, thread and thrum. Make a fresh start, they shout and already you run and have lost your way.

Elusive gateway! Put your arms around me and let my forehead settle among the shining fires . . .

Contrary Currents

You arrived like any guest. With your proud scarf you struck the bottom.

I hid in the darkest corner. I was not frightened but I nursed in my heart a wound that could not heal.

Together we walked in bright daylight. The night was given over to sleep. Each season was a palace hung with brocade and words were minarets from which we called to each other.

Like litanies the clouds pass, the weather changes. Contrary currents, insubstantial dreams, till at last nothing remains for anyone to grasp.

The Kingdom of Heaven is Open

As a last resort, they began to dig: an underground passage from the hilltop where the citadel still stands, winding its way under fields and groves and surfacing roughly one mile south where they could easily attain the pass that crosses the mountain and leads to freedom.

Work progressed quickly. The ground was soft and whenever they encountered rock, they circled it east and west until they were clear of it. Just as the great passageway was finished, the alarm sounded.

In the shade of the far-reaching branches of the old cherrytree you can see the limestone slab where they came up for air. It would take six or eight men to move it. Many years have gone by and no one has moved it but the roots of the old cherry tree perhaps run further and make a more intricate web than those of any other tree in the neighborhood.

A Necessary Burden

'Burst', 'exploded', 'detonated': either of these words might be used but none conveys the exact horror of the German 'platzte' in Georg Büchner's story *Lenz*.

When silence is devoured by its own silence, the soul's center of gravity races through the void. Even as it 'seemed impossible' to the sympathetic observer that the immense crashing sound could have come from the fall of a human being, so the trajectory of that fall is an impossible object of contemplation.

Roommates

A great disorder is an order, it is said. Therefore, half-way up the stairs—the dark, endless seeming spiral of the stairs—my mind is made up. But before I can reach the door, turn the key in the lock, something shapeless, viscous and yet warm and alive rushes past me. Still undefeated, I fling open the door.

'I'll teach you', I say to myself.

The cruelty of these words, the indescribable order of the room.

The Play

He admits to nothing and prefers to remain in the background. She refuses to eat or rather, food has outgrown her although she continues to dress in blue.

I nourish both with stagecraft. Under the glare of diligent projectors, their pale shapes writhe until they bulge gradually, filling the stage and their anger—that prize!—illumines a landscape of scorched plains and cities in ruin.

The Melancholy Man

Don't touch me. Can't you see that my skull is tattooed with resedas and that my skin was shed by a crystal buried beyond remembrance and death? In my hands five or six little fish I have caught leap to the rhythm of my blood.

The Attack

Anger as ice cold water. Plunge your arm into it as far as the elbow. Insensitive stump! As the veins reopen and the fingertips tingle with new life, try to forgive yourself. Gather the nature of your indictment and then . . . O anger, vacant as the calendar's unnumbered days.

St Francis at Dinnertime

for Knud Victor

'Silence, what of silence? Tune up the fine receptors and you'll hear the rabbit sob and sigh like a baby in its dream. Ants are rumbling armies knocking into each other. The spider pulls and flings its sizzling cable through the air and when it walks on its web, it makes a disagreeable sucking sound.'

While he poured the wine, the guests recognized each other by their bright clothes. The bread crumbled and they heard the delicately wrought hammers of agony, doubt, and praise.

Infinitely Small

The infinitely small in infinitely great numbers . . . seraphs, their lips' fervor knows no bounds!

A Voice from the Dream of the Dreamer

A voice from the dream of the dreamer beside me said: I am the dark in the forest, I am also the muddy road, the noise in the underbrush and the tree in which you hide. Catch me, I am the rider whose horse rears on the horizon.

Another voice said: I am the dream within the dream. Not the husk that is shed and falls into oblivion but the field inside the grain, the palace reflected in the mirror inside the palace of mirrors. Catch me, rider and horizon are one.

But the dreamer within the dreamer remained silent. For these pleasures still contained enough charm to erase from his memory all the misfortunes and pain he had suffered. Nothing could rid him of the desire to undertake new travels . . .

The Departure

No sooner had the word been pronounced than I was already standing on the balcony. The cloak rapidly thrown over my shoulders flapped against the iron railing which began to sway. I waved to the group waiting on the street below. When the signal was given, the solid figures dissolved, flooding the pavement as if buckets full had been poured. I looked up at the stars and steered clear of the little reef that jutted out of the waves and had kept traces of human shape.

A Winter's Dream Journal II

30 Poems

I

Not knowing who speaks
Immobility's mobile image
Between four walls diminishing & refracting
This circle is the world

Star burning watery shape
As one asleep is bent
Why there is when she spilled the night
Savage heart

Something instead of nothing
The world and the light
At the entrance of the cave
The triple echo

An oscillating talisman
Headlong into the maze
Trying to remember 'eternal truths'
Clouds in the shape of clouds

Like an incandescence
You wear your skin
Phylacteries with figures inscribed
In June all kinds of flowers

As a thing of words
Erased from the center out
The ubiquitous matchstick strokes
Scintillates & retreats & roots

cavatina 1)

    The moon tonight
    Very simply this time
    Minutest grain in the night's beak
    Over mirror grass

In earthgrasp, in its own shadow's clasp
The position of the scribe
Quiet imparadised precarious disguise quiet
Native place

(and 2)

    Slow slow and stately
    Hymns & odes
    Engrafted on your heart
    The cypresses darkening, sequined

And on their lips
Windows & lamps
Scarce blossom: 'la malicieuse'
The sky constellated fuchsia

ooo

II

Icons, diaphanous tablets
The throat is filled
As line is flame feeding on flame
Who knows its contour

Their blueness, their cushioned hearts
The shelter of the destitute
As antiphon
As pyrope in penumbra

Scintillates & retreats
This circle these leafgreen steps
A star falls back upon itself
Riverbed   grume   scutch

Blinding feathery fiery shedding
Resemblances hung in frames
Powdered lake lasts mouchoir
Ridges: trustworthy tenure

Fragments within blocks of fragments
Most ancient site
Sun dips below ruined parapet stumbling
Overflow and stray   (children

To the farthest edge of sailing
I who deploys
Distance surpassing tide obliterates
Hard by horizon like a flocculence

In monochrome
Cut engenders rainbow run
Nested in sea-ear, mother of pearl
And added

Who'd travel, cross straits
Winter's salvage in us
In a gaze or was glanced at sideways
Suddenly snowpeaks

(19 February, 1988)

High rooms of departure
A hand is poised
As wheel as water the valley the wind's very *pays*
Rushed on, back through the arms of black algae

In the infinite retrenchment of signs
A living image
They appeared once more in the night
Rings, coins' shining corpse

III

Pillar the air almost
And threads, impalpable furrows
Within these precincts
Worlds other ways

The small goods & especially silks store of a language
Suppose you do really dreamspeak
Growing coralline
In which these abound

A kind of excess
Midwinter, winter's bread
Snow flashes and covers the ground late
Its oblique course

In stone in wide in open eyes
Eye argonaut
Between the heart and the throat
Worshipping the light unreasoning reason

The tools, thistles
Time's gold   season & place
Your robe of colors, night, the weight & measure
Glittering leaves; visage

Wind-spired as they are stirred
From the barest field
Full flare unravelled sequence
Fathoming finding lodged expiring

In the opposition of steps
Drawing very close
The naked, knotted sounds
In which space in whose shadowy imprint

. . . is swept the soul
Halfway indelible trace
Bright petals the afternoon
Streaming with the earth unaltered, streamed

As if sucked from its shell the sea
I overheard
In the extreme attention of listening
Your sway

Silence itself   crystal echoes
The dream   the hunt   the flame
Beginning dark and standing wave

oooo

THE LIFELONG RANGE

Suite to A Winter's Dream Journal II

I

the deer's antlers grow like wood

the visible invincible
hip of the thing
        the event

obscure and anxious

        o

a dance of dust

she chases them with a voice

                        in trompe l'oeil

darkened
with birds

        o

small friction clutches
awake at night
a temporary cessation or truce

o

nobody there
on desert roads

a silence would impose itself

                    storms & stones
at varying speeds

o

"we return in the hope of seeing you"

o

I shall answer you with red

        and whilst I breathe the air

in *its* brace entangled

    o

    distinct / unique

"murmurations"!

      cross-
    hatch and swerve

    musick
    A while

    going south
    from the cold

    o

in inked updrafts
swarm starlings   sudden gust
something remembered from earlier
polyphony   shower   child

II

crossing wild woodpaths
crossing
                    lifelong

range 'la flora de Indias'

open to
bitter cane—

in the book of that journey

little stones and hands
on fire

not to be recovered
gaze
barter precious make fast

adversely and enduring

realm remote aftertaste
trust   taste   aftertaste

            o

write threshold write a phrase
unwavering ageing
'I am thinking of you constantly'
the order of events

o

from the center of the earth
phases the moon plaits

A slow surfacing word

o

others so many charms
midmorning chirrups to achieve
four white chained feathery
an air's mastery

o

        unabated tuning

A shape
a shape unshaken

      o

turrets now noon scape
and maze) night's door ajar
dreaming through her disguises
clouds' skill set in thought

January–April 1989

IN THE AVIARY OF VOICES

for Louis

THE NIGHT-ARK

Hast auch du einen Gefallen an uns,
dunkle Nacht ?
        Novalis, *Hymnen an die Nacht*

To

the word-
less, your things'

shadows
stacked against mine

a loose structure
under which we lie

to hold counter-
point

our stunned
voices'

rings, the
prescribed

unquiet
weights.

Fountain

Stone lips
that feed
on stone

their weather-
ing
embrace

final, appeased

for you,
water-addicted
one, breath

our breath
vies
with, stains

the snow
purple.

The Night-Ark

Sea-
rolled, there
where
no blade
propelled,
no whirr,
the sails'—
none of your gulls

no cry
hooked
land, no
branch, greening,
stepped forward—

the night-ark
adrift,
and water-
divided, the
stars.

The Native World

is
like a foreign
country

twitter
in the drab air

the clouds
like swathes

the snake asleep
in its hollow

as the earth
tilts

and the long nights
turn
upon themselves

under
Orion.

Coatlicue's Dream Ritual

When the moon
goddess'

cracked mirror

rises

        you plunge,
flayed,

through your skin's
cloud

already
                dis-
remembering

the body
that meets you

do you cry out, does

dream
cry
out of dream

those
who remain

whisper
among feathers, they
gather shells

listening
to the sound
waves make

to the impeccable
calendar

of blood

of rain mingling.

Night and Silence

with pine-
needled

scarves
two

half-moons'
blanched

and staggered

mask

•

the body of night
and silence

even
night

why
never
even silence

night's
never
silent

painted hive

•

night
after night

withdrawing from

thin dawn of perhaps

....

already the
battlements

those chinked
chattering tree

cherubs

chorister roses, crossroads

.   .   .

Lilith

Lilith of evening
purple stars
secrets to be
talk together

on a hunter's trace

                    God gave
and sent three angels . . .

                    (night-
shade, *belle*
dame,

fond of listening

words from ancient tablets
spearhead
sound into sight

sound's merrythought rosy

beginning

wish would and patience ravish

                    beauty and evil
        flew away

haunts sleepsleep the laughing flower

men in their dreams
the Nile

(milk-
white have seen   a face
        like that of a hawkmoth

a face of memory, a suspending
of time or enchantment.

The Slate Opening

"les pâles figures gravement immobiles"
Gérard de Nerval

I.

Opening slate, your
life

branches
to choose among

An ear for music

•

you sing
for passage

berceuse, lullaby

the beads
coral

. . . from breast
to breast

•

what I loved

as smoke
rises

the wide
night's

plaited
dress, the

honeycomb
of stars

in which
you walked

•

II.

impacted, the
silver
curves

an image
over
the image

as if
through the grain, through

its plied
murmur;

we lent
each other light

phantom evening

•

. . . the voice
at the bottom of the stairs

. . . the sound
of glass shattering

site
of multiple events

variable
mirror

•

in sleep
          we touch, in

its trough

if I   could say to you

'this was the glass, this

blood-
infused word-

shadow,

thread'

•

III.

I would warm
           your mouth

with this glass
nearly full
with ice

and light

………..

when sight is quenched

ghosts, the

ghosts in us, you
           said,

sing

•

waist-
high, stepped

swarm
in drowsiness
the grains, Persephone . . .

hell
and the grape
god are one

meshed fragments, plundered
arms

•

IV.

.......and
that other

transparent
voice

mirror
breathed on, broken:

"the soul
after all, a

woman"

end-
lessly

descends

•

bunched
shadows, bathed

in transparency

as
silk, watered

....

your rings'
new

white
over close-

fitting
green flesh

the morning's
cyclamen

the sea
with all its pennants

. . .

Dune Light

Shadow-
cloths, pinned

and un-
pinned

       settle, again
rise

night-
    drift, its opiate

crests

•

a grain, each night
lodges another

       whispers from further a-
way, from under

glitter debris

•

as when
a morning glory fainteth

                              wind,

    planter, scythe

    your wandering
    drought, your whet-

    stones

                         •

    like voices

    or the hills
              suddenly wavering

                        where
    it diamonds,

              their meeting
    slopes

                         •

    medusas of sand

    each word, once
    murmured,

    grows a shadow

'as the shadow of a great rock
in a weary land'

(Isaiah)

a hiding place

•

not a breath nor bird's cry

merely the cane-brakes'

amphibious, ligatured
lives

persist, still audible

•

foam
made a curtain, was

flood-gate, en-
gaged

where you, it
was you

that went under, entered

•

shivered,

fibrous
and shivered

as the finger
that lights them

in dune
light

       keeping distance
undiminished

•

to drown the lights . . .

as if, deeper

      than
  sleep

the void
unspinning itself, its colors

•

                    towards the wind's edge
          driven

palm-grove
of stars, the

almost rounded
night.

               advancing sand,

you fall,

fall
beyond measure

          .   .   .

Under Sirius

     on heaven's
     neck

     rose
over the crest

the star
              perilous

house
of exaltation

  •

climbed

        instant into instant

as if

             beyond
all drought

  •

           signals,
bleached, immaculate

paths, once
linked

marvelous ladders

•

and their rouged clay
                                        bodies
                loaves
            of myrrh

•

raised

as from a slanted
mirror, the

fragrance

                from their jars

echoed
within

clear, ever in-
accessible

gardens, those

                poured
into glass

●

and the earth, blind,

reckless

      is drawn
            the strain
      of love

●

                fever-

star, burning

      in the thick
      of sleep

          I hear
drilling
itself

into the summer's heart

. . .

IN THE AVIARY OF VOICES

En effet ils furent rois toute une matinée, où les tentures carminées se relevèrent sur les maisons, et toute l'après-midi, où ils s'avancèrent du côté des jardins de palmes.

A. Rimbaud, *Les Illuminations*

Bee Orchis

fluted
up from the root

the Cyclades
in grass, a
hush

of air, of
sky, as
of flight opening

in the pale
glow
of those minute,

wind-
drafted idols.

'A Picture of Perfect Rest'

in memory of Kenneth Rexroth

1.

as
terra sienna

acres
of gold

to Hindustani
dust rust-

colored
gather in

one
loosely

dangling
lantern the

persimmon of
summer's

end
winter's

beginning

2.

'a picture of perfect
rest'

     fruit,

little
stand-still sun

when will you be released

from a growing
transparency

when
          shrink from doom

3.

        contending
till grass
dies

antiphonal
       from trees
so many
        tunes
darting
          so many ways

4.

addressed
to whom

'au monde entier'

delights
in its own

       season's

beginning

'le poème le plus obscur'

5.

no
weave

as October

weaves, its dip-
dyed, ebbing

days

the cherry
tree's

cochineal

laid
over amber

6.

strange expectancies . . .

the staccato
of fieldmice

on dried leaf
avenues

that pass

7.

how keep
the falling season's
light

slopes, summits

      swing back
with their soft shadows

birds
cross
      in straight lines

silence, its
gong

the light
seeds,

escorts

8.

queenly
as precision

the fruit clings to its stem   the end

            brings back the beginning

and it changes

not the heart, the
color

9.

once more

counted
the pale orange trinkets
Pleiad in the half-light

wind
plays with yet moves not

self-enchanted,
pellucid

plays with . . .
moves not . . . words
rounded to fruit fullness,

ice
bringing them sweetness

.   .   .

Dancing Down the Lines . . .

for E. W.

again their drift-
net, the stars'
fruit
and its ripeness
burnished
brief perfect enough
harlequin
sails
the lines
of summer
shot across
imprints
in sand, the
clay flower
charioteer
rouged, petal-
invested
and runway
barely above water.

Li Santo

The saints'
reliquary
roped out of reach

two handfuls
of dust
halved, you

and you

'between'
was what I
unearthed

speak to
where
you, once

touched

•

in the lava bed
glows

rubbed smooth, all
those wishes

the ice
would bud

•

winged niche, a
protuberance

oily with kisses

here, too

our lips
capsized

•

the air
over the salt tablets

as scallop

that the small grain
of loss

I pinned, grow

propitious

•

were the
names

what kept us, made
way

brought
their salt-
weighted
news

.

from mouth
to mouth: pellets

chewed, white mementos . . .

.

some stars, the

slow itineraries

seed-
lings we'd
launched

lighter than, past
our
selves

.

above the whisper-
crypt

chandler, I
as if I dealt myself

light-
free

•

they hardly slept

the glacier stars, only, burning
to the very tips
of their flailed plumage

•

prayer scarves

     'that the images rise
and succeed

one another'

to the precipitous
edge

•

ticked
forward, a

well, it
emptied into itself, a

stone, it
pearled under the lid

even now, even

now

•

against fear
against

the swamp horizons'
furtive
attack: scarp

and counter-
scarp, their
inverted weights

held

•

like a small coin

the key-
stone's hugged,

luminous
rest

•

that, each time
returning, you'd
be

re'invented'

the paled
script

re-
inscribed,

their vagrant, sea-
blown voices
          sound, salt-

cradled

.   .   .

The Butterfly Link

Silvered, the
day breaks at the roof's
rim

pieridae cardamines

in the city dawn

•

are you a soul ship

pitched

between
threshold
and void

drummed

further

and further

from your orchards'
pale children

to have watched them

clambering,

winding
strips of wings

dwindling

and steeped
in green

shrouds

scatter

•

in the air of Provence
in your eyes

agate
and malachite

at the far end of the fragrant terrace

a ship sinks under the moon

•

as if
time

weren't

mountain, its exact
crystals, the hymns

under
ground

    bridge, a single stone's
        reaching, an

      infinite
unaltered

       'yes'   quiet

transparent   châteaux

           •

as when, late
in spring

   above timber and rock

      bristled
with flowers

orchis, the
bee's lip

purple haze over snow

           •

thus turning

      and dipping,

the infrangible
you

chrome-
tipped

      your banners

    the sleeping crystals'

in-
most

      oriflamme

      •

but you,
      have you not seen

love
change

     and light

un-
crested

the red sun

cast
a blood red reflection

shadows of things
                  broken, their

unclaimed
mosaics

          •

day
falters

in bells, all
earth's

dancers, the poem

       . . . *l'amour*
réalisé du désir

while remaining

desire

dormancy of the hills

as if, resonant, in the light
shutting of wings

      • • •

Vignette

. . . no less
than a savage

iron
      killeth

the small, near
         ly

extinct
hours, images

prized

      who plants,
wanders in leafy fields

      those,
banked
with papyri

        a swallow's
wings
ignite, grace

of their passing

        over us, through
us, who are

forms of air, reeved
in air

rise with the prows,
the lunge of crossing.

Summary Diptych

1.

for Tony Baker

when,
and if once you could
reverse the process   day after day
stone after stone   dismantled the shrill
sound of summer   time and space

billows   the sunflower fields in black in gold
dream after dreaming   and where the image
at the eye actually, you say, moves apart

you'd hear the never quiet Book of Hours
now sun   now showered seeds
a sustained vibration or glory

2.

for Anya

                              or swallows / *Schicksalssöhne*
the summer's wheel   decants
                    crimson   blackberry
ash

Ch'ing-chao dreams   words of heaven   winged
chasms in flight   we are who'd stay
                              continually as never
staying behind

the road signals   soar   and deep dive
rivers to raft across
air only rounds

                    Incendiary
the horizon and beginning
                                        frail
flower shadows   ancient   hastening dark

Clear as the Sky over Egypt

I.

idle adorable

grazing on blue

                an instant, a
mere heartbeat's

while it soared,

                    volted

winged helmet
that flowered

of what was this

the dream

we stand on the rock's ledge
casting dice

blue over blue   the peaks, the
              forerunner Alps'

encampments,

flambeaus,

in slow motion extracted
stretches of lives

azul! azul!

in the falcon's cry

the trampling blue

and breaking up of time

II.

on dirait du verre

white
  coral beaches

the imagined and light of language

 pyramidal
light

chance reeling birds hasp,
       talons & wings

  a plain that's bright
      to look on

from the hills

    In reality & in dreams

  as if pitching, engaged
 with glass

glass caravel *en route* the sails

  are motionless

in the noonlight, its
formidable branching

murmur of the shore, distinct

the clouds beyond

III.

again between boundaries

leaf to leaf

              mother musician,
morning's Eve

springs to light

in the color of things

spider floss trails

the first measure's

airy

marine rose

surges

                bewegt

            langsam
              bewegt

the song line

it raises
           thick, thick the leaves

faith

            that

                         'greenhouse

kept me
warm prisoner
of war I

      sang'

IV.

and

Joan Miró

from the farm in Montroig: "... *quelques*
petits points de couleur, un arc-

en-

ciel"

years
    later

painted
the blue triptych

its blue hanging in the trees blue

its blue shadows over eyes blue

its blue hands caressing, knowing blue

our blue bodies pressed against
                  branch bound to leaf, sounding blue

the lines'
giddiness
invades, flows
into July

red purple scent

                          the immortelles
stacked in their gold

in another glance

in a summer morning

are poised

. . .

In the Aviary of Voices

Someone

    it wasn't you

said

Hello!   Hello!

I could have killed
you

    invisible, invisible
    you

•

ambushed, I grow

    feathers
    in my throat

one
by one, I pluck them

while you

    fly
    safe

        under the suave
plumage

•

in the aviary of voices

we speak the language   the same

in and out/between staves

that

never touch   we

tear

•

the trajectory within

memory

is space reconstituted   with 'masks'

striae
over a blotted mouth

•

cry out   did you

I

as far   as

archipelago   sea-wedge, echo-

    less

       •

    from the center

      "kill"

a cleavage   devours

     this passion

      •

    I carry like a white fruit

what blinds me

       no one   not even

you

    at arm's length, ir-
    reversible

      •

the irregular progression of   forget-

fulness roots
in the eyes, beginning
there

gulls

on bare islands: *"mon amour! mon amour!"*

                                        as white
                                        on white

                                                        obliterates.

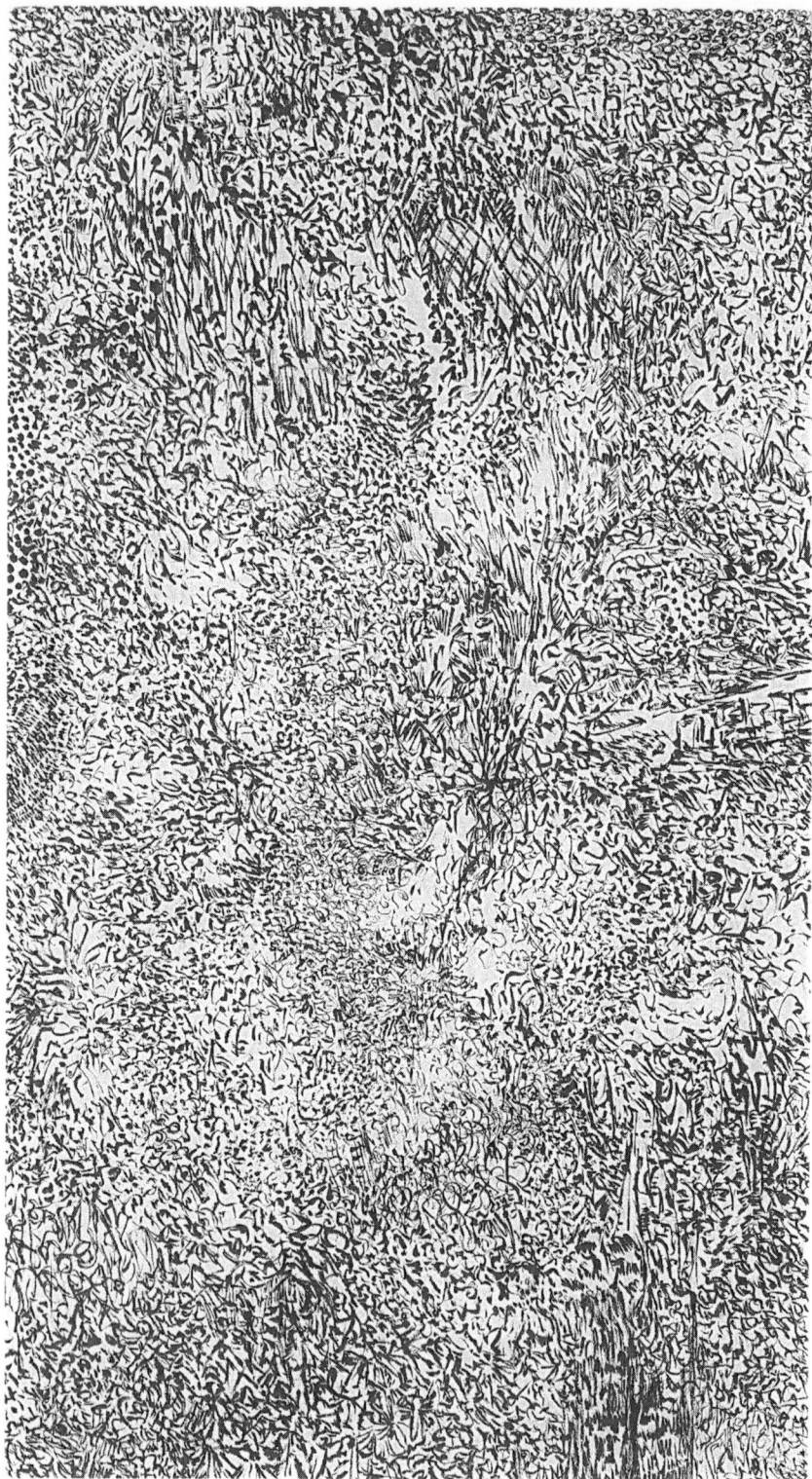

Yunnan Sketches

for Karen H.

I. Tiger Leaping Gorge

beginning with a children's song from the *Shi-ching*
(*Book of Songs*, Arthur Waley's translation)

The Little Lady of Ch'ing-Ch'i

Her door opened on the white water
Close by the side of the timber bridge;
That's where the little lady lived
All alone without a lover.

Your door opened on the white water
Close by the leaping stone
A stranger in the land
Alone with your anxious heart.

The roaring stream below, snow peaks above
Curve after curve, the mountain road
Thinking of the prince who went wandering
And did not return.

High, high above, my friend
At ease among the snow peaks
Without thought of going back
Ready to float up to the clouds.

With this mountain-grass broom
I, too, would join the immortals
It got lost along the way
There's nothing left to do but wait.

Sun rising behind Jade Dragon
Sun setting behind Mount Haba
Deep in the gorge, unobserved
Flinging stones into the rapids below.

Sheer rock faces closing in, inch-wide the sky
Sudden silence; where did the river go?
Intruding upon a spirit world
We ought to tread as on thin ice.

Tread as on thin ice, muffle the heartbeat
With luck we'll clear the passage
Painted bright, face to face
Awe and dread guard house and temple gate.

What are you doing here, child, alone
High up by the dust road?
Grandma's down in the drop
Where healing grasses grow . . .

Wait, wait, little boy,
She will surely return!

At *full stars* site, dashing spray
Travellers stop to gaze, time passing on—
Here, in these living eyes, I see
Waiting still, another lonely, towering form.

Gorge narrowing, gorge opening up again
Green water crashing, white water leaping
Arms or hearts, which is the more violent
I cannot say.

With prayer-bead words, with streamer clouds
With the remembered line, with the forgotten poems
With everything inscribed, with everything washed away
With a long way yet to White Face Peak Refuge.

Waking up in the shadow of White Face Peak
So close, close almost to touch—
Yet its crevices run so deep
Nothing could thread them green nor grief soothe.

* * *

Not really, really a *château* but a mountain lodge
Not really hermit poets musing, tranquil and grand
Mist, plus pavilion, plus lake—mostly polluted—
Just us, prince and queens having breakfast.

. . . and for crown jewels, seeds
From the castor-oil tree
Three to plant—will grow or not—three to keep
For delight.

Bright little colts, so smart in your snap-shot gear!
Should an offer to ride
Straight into the tomb of some unfortunate princess
Be declined?

Though I, too, would love a dress of pure jade
I count the years left, some bleak, some bright
And the horses of my suite
I'd rather see trotting beside me on the mountain road.

In the river, reflected, a dress of jade
I count the floating peaks, the years
And the horses of my suite
Trotting beside me on the mountain road.

If the stone drum were struck
Could it be heard deep in third gorge?
At first bend, laughing and shouting
Here we tread lightly, make haste.

Laughing and shouting, who cares?
Birds on the dance-floor sand in March
Tracing the characters for 'gold' and 'sand'
The June rains will sweep clear.

It's getting late by *miracle lake*
For two hours people fished—caught plenty
Then the torrent broke through the landslide
Where do we cross over?

With this kind of craft
With no landing in sight—
Smoke for luck!
No choice but trust.

As leaf on current
By counter-current clasped
In midstream
Ever floats all care out of the world.

Sun setting, blue stars pouring
Down over Eastern Slope
Raise your cup to all flowers
Raise your eyes to the dragon clouds.

* * *

II. North and South

Full moon and hearts, people crowd close
What will the artist make of a face?
How extravagant, that missing tooth
Beside flowering pink almond.

Pink peach, white pear
Follow each other in bloom
Qing Qing's needles clatter
Variably, in and out of tune

      (her curiosity can't be helped).

Green green the fern
Red red the yarn
Double stitches single hearts
Retain.

Walking straight ahead, straight road, curving road
Doubting nothing, *boundless and free*
With the three hundred sixty-five feathered bird
Among the moving white mists of spring.

After lunch—not even a short nap
Off to visit famous Doctor Ho—
For those regretting the day's shortness or tiring of the year's sloth
Does he grow the herb *devoid of joy or sadness*?

Snow mountain flowers and a monkey's heart
                              grow old together in a glass jar
Pale yellow orchids and crimson vine twist up to the eaves
Neighbors stop by, share a puff of smoke
May the mountains forever protect *full box* village.

No fishing, no boats on Dian Lake
Emperors had their say; they're dead—
Yet how fine-looking this old man
Who gently touches the turtle of long life.

Swallows dart over black tiles
Earth-brown houses by the rushing stream
The water-buffalo takes his ease, drinks slow and deep
The hills alive with white worms.

"War is on", says Mr. Horse
We drive on South . . . wildflowers
So lovely at first: "invader weeds"
Alongside empty Ho Chi Minh Road.

No poems on flowered paper, no gold locks on the double doors
Two pillows embroidered for the guest
Sweet and fresh the night air in Zhu Family Mansion
A cricket singing its heart out, at the edge of heaven.

Orion breaks clear, Rigel and Betelgeuse in place
The courtyard fragrant with rain
A lone silhouette bars the window without blinds
In the oval mirror, a single stroke.

Where dragons on satin sleep on the South sky-line
Of rosewood the beds, by eaves' wing the city gate
By Red Mud River we turn, up the double-cloud path
With dreams kept close as pomegranate its seeds.

The air, a dance-floor in the late afternoon sun
And you can't detach your eyes from it
The hills flatten and the shadows grow
Cold jewels, cold jewels.

Waiting for the day lilies to open
Now that you know their secret meaning
If only for a day, *sorrow-forgotten*
Would spread, spring after spring.

March–June, 2003

Notes to 'Yunnan Sketches'

page 191. For the prince's story, see Ch'u Tzu: *The Songs of the South* in David Hawkes' translation (Oxford: Oxford University Press, 1959), p.119.

page 192. Jade Dragon Snow Mt. (5,596m / 18,360 ft) and Haba Snow Mt. (5,396m / 17,703 ft). Jade Dragon Snow Mountain has 13 snow-covered peaks.

— "At *full stars* site": the last line refers to a poem by Su Tung-p'o, 'The Husband Watching Height' (1059) translated by Burton Watson, (*Selected Poems of Su Tung-p'o*, Port Townsend, WA: Copper Canyon Press, 1995).

page 193. The "unfortunate princess" referred to is Princess Yongtai of the imperial court. She died in 701, at the age of 19, in childbirth, or was condemned to death by her grandmother, the Empress Wu, because of some reported remark. Yongtai's father, who next ascended the throne, gave her and her husband a grand burial. Her tomb, discovered near Xian, contained 777 ceramic figurines of soldiers, servants, hunters and courtiers, as well as camels and horses.

page 193–4. In the Han period tomb of Prince Liu Sheng and his consort Dou Wan (2nd century B.C.), the corpses discovered were encased from head to toe in over 2000 plaques of jade, sewn together with gold thread.

page 194. The stone drum at Shigu, along the first bend of the Yangtze, commemorates a Sino-Naxi victory over the Tibetans in 1548.

— "miracle lake": In 1996 an earthquake not only destroyed sections of Dayan (Old Lijiang), taking several lives, but here in the gorge caused an entire mountainside to slide down into the Jin Sha (Yangtze), creating a lake full of trapped fish.

page 196. "devoid of joy or sadness": from a poem called 'After Lunch' by Po Chü-I (772–846), in the translation by Arthur Waley (London: George Allen & Unwin, 1946).

page 197. "War is on." That day, the U.S. Army invaded Iraq.

— "No poems . . .": see the poem 'To the Tune "The Perfumed Garden"' by Li Ch'ing Chao (1084–1151), translated by Kenneth Rexroth and Ling Chung (Li Ch'ing Chao: *Complete Poems*. New York: New Directions, 1979).

SONNET SEQUENCE

I.

like the spider I eat yesterday's web
to make today's like the branches
stripped of their leaves I grow dark
with rain wind shakes me

through and through polishing
to flint sheen the flux reflux of shadows
I carry myself on air
testing my weight light on the instant's curve

I remember all the names
their phosphorescent peaks
extinguished stars

they chill upon the ground
line after hair-thin line
with the ascending dark.

II.

> "They went to live in the island
> Once called Loveliest"
> —Pindar, *Pythian* IV

on white-washed Thera
our shadows are beautiful
figures in a dance
passers-by take no notice

there is no record
of bare feet on barley grass
the thud of bare feet on the barley grass
the jars are empty

in the violet hour
in the hour of the last departure
griffins stir winged shadows

the cliff plunges deeper into the sea
a tug-boat circles toy running silver
anemones close upon ash.

III.

what catches the eye
is now an elusive image
in Santa Maria della Grazie
the scalpel inches away

while the cheap ring
you wear with grace
is singleness contained
unaffected by what might have been

uninjured you abstain
from doing—on the curvature of space
things as they are

retrieve a magnificence submerged
the size of your smallest fingernail
a chip of Leonardo.

IV.

no bells from Maguelone
water-ensouled the childless
winter-gray enfolds
expands expanding waste

no pilgrim lights
in driftwood's salt-
scooped heart the ascending
salt takes root

there is no staying here no one to save
no hourglass healing sounds'
blond magic held in air

in Maguelone's embrace
where like a winter bird passed through
acanthus grows a forest wreath.

V.

the late late late rose bends
perception of the rose
consciousness of the rose
locked within its prism

the cost of loss of the rose
the precise count
the rose coined generous
assembled from pure air rose

triggered the bowstring rose
to exquisite mouth-in-death
was the same rose in a flash

was wind as it swept your face
to where leaves lie thick
in the fading light in the autumn rain.

VI.

"wrapt in the wave of that music"
—W.B.Yeats

what effort knots to a choir
fills your house empties the corners of morning
in time with its measure its music
keeps as a fan fuels desire

as salt fierce on snow the future past mourning
as motionless as the day occasioned by music
you'd walk with these voices on air
sharpen them blade on stone

moss rebounds relinquishes nothing
but a phantom that feeds on that nothing
a thing yet to be born a present furled there

now effort and choruses ended the salt on the snow thrown
the folds of the motionless fan folded to soothing
at a wrist's turn to flourish the losing.

VII.

The Hearse

green lighter than emerald
spring green in fall's season
stood folded infolding dispatch
between vineyard and the green wood

stood while drop drop implacable
time rose in dulled rhythm
from the earth-room shaft birth-room
not-to-be-crossed-again threshold

arched there then from sight moved out of hearing
diminutive as through glass
as light on leaf turning

from sight out of hearing
diamond dreamt of, a ravishment
or bridal perhaps, sealed.

Breinigsville, PA USA
15 December 2010
251456BV00001B/7/P

9 781848 611313